Katherine Applegate *illustrated by* G. Brian Karas

IVAN

A Gorilla's True Story

CLARION BOOKS

Houghton Mifflin Harcourt

Boston | New York

Special thanks to: Jody Gripp and Jean Fisher, Special Collections/Northwest Room, Tacoma Public Library; Diane Allen, Liberty High School, Renton, WA; Mark Coleman, PAWS, Lynnwood, WA; and Jodi Carrigan, Zoo Atlanta.

Clarion Books
3 Park Avenue
New York, New York 10016

Text copyright © 2014 by Katherine Applegate
Illustrations copyright © 2014 by G. Brian Karas

Clarion Books is an imprint of Houghton Mifflin Harcourt Publishing Company.

hmhbooks.com

Cover design by Jessica Handelman
Interior design by Christine Kettner

Library of Congress Cataloging-in-Publication Data is available.
LCCN: 2013043952

ISBN 978-0-544-25230-1 (hardcover)
ISBN 978-0-358-41746-0 (paper over board)

Manufactured in China
SCP 10 9 8 7 6 5 4 3 2 1
4500794925

For everyone who loved Ivan

In leafy calm,
in gentle arms,
a gorilla's life began.

The baby was born in a tropical forest
in central Africa.

He was part of a large family
of western lowland gorillas.

The troop included babies,
juveniles,
females,
and a male leader,
the silverback.

The more the baby gorilla grew,
the more he played.
The more he played,
the more he learned.

He rode on his mother's back.
He listened to the hoots
and grunts
and chest-beats
of his father.
He watched the older gorillas,
clever and quick,
as they wrestled and chased
and swung from vines.

He did not learn about humans
until it was too late.

Poachers with loud guns
and cruel hands
stole the little gorilla
and another baby.

After thousands of miles
and endless days
in a black, damp crate,
at last came light
and fresh air.

The jungle, green with life,
was gone.

The gorillas had traveled
halfway around the world
to Tacoma, Washington.
A man who owned a shopping mall
had ordered and paid for them,
like a couple of pizzas,
like a pair of shoes.

People cooed and laughed
and held the babies.

They dressed them
in human clothes

and fed them
human food.

The shopping mall owner
ran a "Name the Babies" contest.
The winning names were
Burma and Ivan.

One dark day
soon after the babies arrived
in their strange new world,
Burma died.
Without her,
Ivan was all alone,
with too much left to learn.

While he was little,
Ivan was cute and cuddly.
For three years he lived in a home
like a human child.

He slept in a bed

and went to baseball games.

He held babies
and rode on a
motorcycle.

He had to learn many things
gorillas in the wild
don't ever need to know.

The one thing Ivan didn't need to learn
was how to eat.
The more he ate, the more he grew.
The more he grew, the less he could live
a human life
in a human house.

A cage in the mall
became Ivan's new home.
There wasn't much to do.

 Sometimes Ivan
watched TV.

Sometimes he played
with an old tire.

 Sometimes he finger-painted,
signing the papers
with his thumbprint.

Mostly, he watched the humans
watching him.

Ivan was about thirteen
when his coat began to shimmer
with silvery-white hairs.
He'd grown into a silverback gorilla.
In the jungle,
he would have been ready
to protect his family.

But he had no family
to protect.

Year after year passed.

People began to grow angry
about Ivan's lonely life.
Children and adults wrote letters,
and signed petitions,
and held protests.

Ivan lived in his cage

without the company of other gorillas

for twenty-seven years

before he was sent

on another journey.

This time the hands were gentle.

Zoo Atlanta
wasn't a jungle.
It was a place with walls.
Still, the breeze carried
jungle sounds and scents.

Scientists who understood
the needs of gorillas
helped Ivan adjust
slowly,
carefully,
gently
to his new life.

Finally, it was time.

Was Ivan ready?

Cameras clicked.

Reporters watched.

When Ivan stepped onto the cool green grass,

the sunlight gleaming on his silver hair,

people cheered

and laughed

and wept with joy.

Ivan,

the shopping mall gorilla,

was in a place with trees

and grass

and other gorillas

at last.

In leafy calm,

in gentle arms,

a gorilla's life began

again.